# Colin Kaepernick: The Inspiring Story of One of Football's Greatest Quarterbacks

An Unauthorized Biography

By: Clayton Geoffreys

Copyright © 2015 by Clayton Geoffreys

All rights reserved. Neither this book nor any portion thereof may be reproduced or used in any manner whatsoever without the express written permission. Published in the United States of America.

**Disclaimer**: The following book is for entertainment and informational purposes only. The information presented is without contract or any type of guarantee assurance. While every caution has been taken to provide accurate and current information, it is solely the reader's responsibility to check all information contained in this article before relying upon it. Neither the author nor publisher can be held accountable for any errors or omissions.

Under no circumstances will any legal responsibility or blame be held against the author or publisher for any reparation, damages, or monetary loss due to the information presented, either directly or indirectly. This book is not intended as legal or medical advice. If any such specialized advice is needed, seek a qualified individual for help.

Trademarks are used without permission. Use of the trademark is not authorized by, associated with, or sponsored by the trademark owners. All trademarks and brands used within this book are used with no intent to infringe on the trademark owners and only used for clarifying purposes.

This book is not sponsored by or affiliated with the National Football League, its teams, the players, or anyone involved with them.

Visit my website at www.claytongeoffreys.com

Cover photo by Mike Morbeck is licensed under CC BY 2.0 / modified from original

# Table of Contents

Foreword ..................................................................... 1

Chapter 1: Childhood and Early Life ........................... 3

Chapter 2: High School Years ..................................... 9

Chapter 3: College Years at the University of Nevada ..... 18

    Freshman Year ..................................................... 18

    Sophomore Year ................................................... 22

    Junior Year ........................................................... 25

    Senior Year ........................................................... 29

    MLB ..................................................................... 33

Chapter 4: Kaepernick's NFL Career ......................... 39

    The Draft .............................................................. 41

    2012 Season: Kaepernick's Emergence ................ 48

    2013 Season: The Seahawk Roadblock ............... 57

    2013 Regular Season ........................................... 61

    2014 Season: A Step in the Wrong Direction ...... 66

Chapter 5: Colin Kaepernick's Legacy and Future ........... 76

Final Word/About the Author ............................................ 79

Bibliography ....................................................................... 83

# Foreword

Colin Kaepernick has quickly established himself as a quality quarterback in today's National Football League. Since receiving his opportunity to start towards the middle of the 2012 season, Kaepernick has become a steady quarterback averaging over three thousand yards a season between 2013 and 2014. Though still incredibly young at the time of this writing, Kaepernick has demonstrated consistency in his abilities as a starting quarterback. As of September 2015, he continues to hold the record for most rushing yards by a quarterback in the postseason. Thank you for downloading *Colin Kaepernick: The Inspiring Story of One of Football's Greatest Quarterbacks*. In this unauthorized biography, we will learn Colin's incredible life story and impact on the game of football. Hope you enjoy and if you do, please do not forget to leave a review! Also, check out my website at claytongeoffreys.com to join my exclusive list where I let you know about my latest books and give you goodies!

Cheers,

*Clayton Geoffreys*

*Visit me at [www.claytongeoffreys.com](www.claytongeoffreys.com)*

## Chapter 1: Childhood and Early Life

On November 3, 1987, Colin Kaepernick was born to his biological mother, 19-year-old Heidi Russo from Milwaukee, Wisconsin. Russo was single and did not belong to the wealthy families in the city. His father, on the other hand, was long gone before little Colin was brought to the world. Colin is a biracial baby who shared the traits of his Caucasian mother and African-American father.

At the time Russo gave birth to Colin, she wasn't ready. She was just barely out of high school and is not ready for the responsibilities involved in taking care for another human being. Thus, she put up little Colin for adoption. The family who adopted Colin turned out to be a family who wants a young healthy boy. The couple actually made many attempts that ended in heartbreak.

Rick and Teresa Kaepernick had lost two sons very early in life. The first was Lance, who died when he was 23 days old. Those first few days had so much optimism when he was brought home. However, it turned out that he has a serious heart defect that led to two open heart surgeries, but still, he did not survive. Their second son was little Kent who didn't last as long when he battled a heart defect. He died when he was just four days old.

The couple eventually became successful in their next two attempts, which gave them two healthy children in a daughter, Devon, and a son, Kyle. Despite having a healthy son and daughter, the couple still wanted another child. However, the doctors had warned them that another attempt would be too risk for Teresa. It is important to note that at that time, in the late 80s, the technology in the medicine was not as advanced as it is today.

Kent and Teresa adopted Colin from the Lutheran Social Services in Appleton, Wisconsin. He was a healthy and vibrant little boy who had a lot of life in him. Colin does not have a memory of his birth mother. In an interview with the Associated Press in 2013, he expressed his lack of desire to meet his mother. Kent and Teresa did not treat Colin as an adopted son. Rather they treated him like he is a real part of their family.

Growing up, Colin was a biracial child growing up in a white household and it didn't seem to affect the people within the home. The parents never made any effort to hide the fact that he was adopted and that his skin color was different from both his parents and the siblings. Despite the obvious difference, it never was a big deal for Colin.

Colin was the youngest of three children who spent their early years living in Fond du Lac, Wisconsin. It is a small town with less than 50,000 people that is located in the southeastern part of the state. When Colin was just four-years-old, they moved to Turlock,

California when his father, Kent Kaepernick, accepted an executive role at the Hilmar Cheese Company.

What's interesting about Turlock is that some of the known professional athletes have come from this little town – including former Oakland Raider, Lester Hayes, who won two Super Bowl rings in 1981 and 1984. Other notable athletes to came from Turlock include Alison Cox (Olympic swimmer), Brad Lesley (MLB, Cincinnati Reds and Milwaukee Brewers), Tommy Mendonca (MLB, Philadelphia Phillies), and Tony Corbin (NFL, Arena Football, and Canadian Football League). However, the young Colin didn't show signs of achieving success as a professional athlete in his early years. In fact, he didn't start throwing the football right away.

Colin's parents introduced him to a youth football league when he was eight years old when the family moved to Turlock, California. The first snaps young Kaepernick would take wouldn't be as the quarterback he is known for. Instead, he was used as a defensive end and a punter – rarely getting any time on the field. It was not until one year later that he was given a shot to try his hand and arm at being a quarterback.

Just like how the old saying goes, first impressions are often the best, and young Colin's first ever throw in a youth game resulted to a long-distance touchdown. His mother, Teresa, stated in an interview with the New York Times in 2010, that the parents who were sitting in the stands were in utter surprise and disbelief - with many sitting with their mouths wide open. At that time it became evident that there was something special in this this average nine-year-old Colin, who hardly attempted a pass.

That arm would also be noticed when he grew up playing more than just football as he also developed his skills on the baseball field. Both sports would display his various athletic strengths. He continued to develop his skills as a quarterback on the football field he also pitched on the baseball diamond.

Who knows what would have happened if Colin's mother didn't bring him to an adoption center in a small town in Wisconsin? Nevertheless, Colin was destined for great things, and his parents were supporting him – regardless if they were adoptive and not related by blood. Colin would participate and win several punt, pass, and kick competitions as a child, often throwing the ball over the heads of the officials who were not expecting to have to go very far to retrieve the ball.

## Chapter 2: High School Years

Colin Kaepernick continued to develop his overall athleticism by becoming a three-sport athlete at Pitman High School in Turlock. He played football in the fall, basketball in the winter, and baseball in the spring. Two of the three would eventually become his standout sports.

Kaepernick didn't have to do much as a quarterback at first. In fact, the Pride was known as a running team with a few powerful backs. In his game as a starter on September 9, 2004, Kaepernick only had five attempts with two completions – one of which was a 21-yard pass for a first quarter touchdown. But the team was led by junior-back Anthony Harding's 233 yards, and senior-back Mark Runyan's 117 yards as Pitman combined for 471 rushing yards in a 46-36 win at home against Kennedy High School (Sacramento).

One week later, Kaepernick began to show how good of an arm he had when he went 14-for-20 for 203 yards and three touchdowns in a 19-7 victory over Johansen High School (Modesto) on September 17, 2004.

The games would flip between whether the Pride would focus more on the rushing attack, or let Kaepernick have the opportunities to throw. His final numbers at the end of the season were 1,051 passing yards, 13 touchdowns, and four interceptions. Kaepernick helped the Pitman Pride to an 8-3 record in his junior season that ended on November 19, 2004 against West High School from Tracy, California - a state playoff game where they lost 35-21. Kaepernick was 14-for-27 for 171 yards, one touchdown, and one interception.

In his senior season, Kaepernick would be given more chances to throw the ball as his overall numbers increased to 1,954 passing yards with 25 touchdowns against six interceptions. There were games where he looked really good and others where he looked somewhat average, which is a big part of why he wasn't initially getting scholarship offers from Division I Football Bowl Subdivision programs.

In his first game as a senior against Granite Bay High School on September 9, 2005, Kaepernick was 13-for-24 for 170 yards and three touchdowns, but he also had two interceptions that resulted to a season-opening loss of 40-39. After that, he was much more efficient and didn't throw an interception in the next five games – a streak that included a 56-20 victory over Ceres High School on September 23, 2005, where Kaepernick was eight-for-12 for 139 yards. Half of his completions were touchdown passes.

The team would then face the West Wolf Pack from Tracy, who eliminated them from the state playoffs last year. On November 25, 2005, West would win again by a score of 27-22 over Pitman – Kaepernick played well with 11-for-14 passes for 180 yards and two touchdowns. Overall, he would finish his career with 3,005 passing yards, 38 touchdowns and only 10 interceptions.

There were some concerns with how he would do if he ever translated to the world of college football. In the summer prior to his senior year at Pitman, Kaepernick was entered into a number of college football camps where he showed his skills in person in an attempt to entice some of the best college programs in the area.

He was invited to attend one camp at Boise State University in Idaho, who were starting to become a national powerhouse out of the smaller Mountain West Conference. However they didn't bite and on his way back to Turlock, he made a visit to attend a football camp for the University of Nevada where he was one of the 18 quarterbacks being given a series of exercises in what was essentially a tryout. Kaepernick debuted in similar fashion as when he threw in his first youth game nearly 10 years prior. He showed he had the strongest arm despite a throwing motion that left some to be desired.

But strong arms are a gift while the technique to throw a football properly could be developed with coaching. Thus, the Nevada Wolfpack program offered him a scholarship to play. It was where he would do well in football. However, there was a moment while attending Pitman that he almost found himself playing a different sport after high school.

He was a standout on the baseball diamond as he had developed a 94-mile-per-hour fastball to help the Pitman Pride varsity pitching staff during his junior and senior years – an impressive feat for any young and talented baseball prospect. In his junior year in 2005, Kaepernick pitched in 10 starts with seven complete games where he compiled a season earned runs average (ERA) of 1.54 and a 6-4 record.

One of his best games was in a May 4, 2005 victory over Los Banos where Pitman won 4-1. Kaepernick allowed only three hits and no earned runs with 14 strikeouts. One week later, he would collect another 13 strikeouts in a complete game win 3-1 over inner-city rival Turlock High School on May 11, 2005.

In addition to his strong pitching arm, he was pretty decent at the plate with a .325 batting average in 27 games. But his numbers overall would look a lot stronger in his senior season as he helped the Pitman Pride finish the season 26-6-1. It was the year where he would have two no-hitters in the year.

The first no-hitter came on March 10 in a 7-1 win against Hilmar High School where Kaepernick had 15 dominating strikeouts – thanks to his 94-miles-per-hour fastball. However, he had four walks to cost him the shutout. A few weeks later, on March 29, 2006, against Los Banos High School, Kaepernick would throw a complete seven inning with eight strikeouts against three walks for a 5-0 victory.

14

At the end of his senior season, Kaepernick finished with a record of 9-2 and an ERA of only 1.27, combined with 97 strikeouts and 39 walks. After sweeping Tokay High School (Lodi) on May 24-26, the Pride was swept by Elk Grove High School, losing 8-1 on May 31, 2006, and 4-2 on June 3, 2006.

In the final game of his high-school career, Kaepernick gave up four runs on eight hits. While he only had one scholarship offer for football from Nevada, he had plenty of college baseball offers waiting for him from Notre Dame University, the University of Tennessee, and Arizona State University. He would continue playing baseball in the spring at Nevada, where he was offered a chance to play football in the fall for the Wolfpack.

Some might wonder how Colin did on the basketball court. He wasn't bad, but he was definitely better suited for playing football and baseball – and making basketball a sport better used for keeping active in-between seasons. However, he played a total of 54 games for the Pride as a varsity player in his junior and senior seasons – averaging 13.8 points per game.

One would wonder how well he did in the classroom, considering the workload of being a three-sport athlete. Kaepernick was known for having a dedicated work ethic, not only on the field of play, but also in the classroom. In fact, in a feature on *Sports on Earth*, his teachers shared a number of stories that supported how he was a well-rounded student-athlete.

The article mentioned how he met with his counselor upon entering his senior year with a weighted 4.3 grade point average. He was not going to have any trouble meeting the academic standards the NCAA requires when wanting to earn a scholarship to play football at the next level. Usually, most seniors want to have an open period to either come in late in the morning or get an extra period for studying. However, Kaepernick didn't want to just settle and have an easy route to a straight-A report card – so he took what was available in that period to fill the open slot. He took Psychology.

# Chapter 3: College Years at the University of Nevada

## Freshman Year

Colin Kaepernick entered the 2007 football season as a redshirt freshman for the University of Nevada Wolfpack team. His real freshman year at Nevada started in the fall of 2006 but was kept off the team to prepare to start his eligibility in 2007. However, he wouldn't see a lot of game action at first with sophomore quarterback Nick Graziano returning to help build on an 8-5 record from the previous year. Graziano was the one selected to replace Jeff Rowe after his graduation.

It was a rough start to the season with a 52-10 loss to Nebraska on September 1, 2007, where Graziano only had eight completions out of his 24 passing attempts for only 109 yards and one interception. Kaepernick had some time to throw a few passes, but only had one completion for negative yardage.

He would watch from the sidelines as the Wolfpack went on the road to play Northwestern in Illinois on October 8, 2007. Graziano showed why he was selected to start the season with 377 passing yards and two touchdowns against one interception. Nevada was able to get the win over Nichols State with 52-17 where Kaepernick had just one completion for 12 yards and an interception in the late minutes of a blowout.

Kaepernick would see his minutes increase almost instantly on October 6, 2007, in a home game against the Fresno State Bulldogs. Even though the team lost 49-41, the Wolfpack found they may have found something special in a quarterback who was redshirted in the previous season. Graziano suffered a broken foot in the second quarter and Kaepernick had to fill-in. There were a lot of questions, which is common for any true freshman quarterback being thrown into the game unexpectedly. There also weren't a lot of ringing endorsements considering his lackluster performance in those first three games.

However, Kaepernick was able to handle the pressure by putting up some pretty big numbers, considering he played for a little more than a half of football with 23-for-36 for 384 yards and four touchdowns, as well as 60 yards and one touchdown while rushing the ball. In fact, Kaepernick made some big plays late in the fourth quarter despite the comeback falling short.

Nevada was able to complete a drive late in the fourth quarter that ended with a 36-yard touchdown pass from Kaepernick to Luke Lippincott. After an onside kick recovery, Kaepernick was able to lead another touchdown drive when completing a 34-yard touchdown pass to Adam Bishop with three seconds left.

Kaepernick was able to show he wasn't a one-hit wonder as he had another dominating performance against the Boise State Broncos. Although they lost

69-67 in a four-overtime game, he was able to complete 11 passes for 243 yards and three touchdowns, including a 58-yard touchdown pass to Marko Mitchell in the second quarter. His legs were a big asset for the Wolfpack as he rushed for 177 yards on the ground with two touchdowns – a 9-yard run into the end-zone to keep the game close in the fourth quarter to keep the game tied, and then another 25-yard run to keep Nevada in the game in the second overtime.

The only reason Nevada lost was a not completed two-point conversion to match what Boise State was able to do in their fourth-overtime drive. But despite the even 6-6 record, Kaepernick was playing very efficiently to finish the season with 53.8 percent completions, 2,175 yards, 19 touchdowns, and only three interceptions. He also ran with the ball 105 times for 593 rushing yards and six touchdowns.

With a 6-6 record, the Wolfpack was still eligible for a post-season appearance in the New Mexico Bowl on December 22, 2007. But Kaepernick and the Nevada team ran into a bit of a figurative brick wall in a 23-0 shutout loss, with a total of only 210 yards on offense. Kaepernick had only 137 passing yards on 13-of-31 passing and only 26 yards on 12 carries.

In the end, Kaepernick won the Western Athletic Conference's Freshman of the Year Award and also received an honorable mention on the 2007-2008 All-American team roster. The Nevada coaching staff also awarded him the Fireman's Award –for stepping in when he was called to fill an important void. This led to a little bit of a quarterback controversy when Kaepernick returned for his sophomore season with Graziano returning from his foot injury.

**Sophomore Year**

Kaepernick would display his skills through his arm and feet in his sophomore season after beating out

Graziano. It started with three rushing touchdowns in the season-opening victory over visiting Grambling State (49-13) – with 7- and 19-yard touchdown runs in the first quarter and a 28-yard score in the third quarter before getting the rest of the game off.

After that, the Wolfpack struggled in a 35-19 loss to Texas Tech on September 6, 2008, and in a 69-17 road loss to the Missouri Tigers on September 13, 2008. But Kaepernick would find his groove again as Nevada bounced back with a 49-27 win on September 27, 2008 over in-state rival UNLV. It was a game where Kaepernick stood out with 240 rushing yards and three touchdowns that were highlighted by a 66-yard run to start the second half. He also threw 11-for-16 for 176 yards and two passing touchdowns.

In the next game on October 4, 2008, Kaepernick would throw 19 completions out of 24 attempts for 243 yards through the air and two touchdowns against the Idaho Vandals in a 49-14 road win in Moscow, Idaho.

Kaepernick put up a lot of numbers and became one of only a few quarterbacks who would join the 2,000-yard passers and 1,000-yard rushes after finishing the season with 2,849 passing yards and 22 touchdowns against seven interceptions. He also had 1,130 yards on the ground with 17 touchdowns.

Beyond the win over UNLV, Kaepernick's best performances on the ground came from a three-game series that went from late October to early November. On October 25, 2008, the Wolfpack lost 38-31 to Hawaii on the road, but Kaepernick had 139 yards and one touchdown along with 173 passing yards and two more touchdowns. He would score a total of four rushing touchdowns after running for 118 and two scores against Fresno State (November 7, 2008), and 147 yards against San Jose State (November 15, 2008). Nevada won both games as key parts of their improved 7-6 record that brought the Wolfpack back to Boise, Idaho, for the Humanitarian Bowl on December 30, 2008. It was a 42-35 loss where Kaepernick had 370 yards on 24-for-47 throws for three touchdowns and two interceptions.

## Junior Year

In his junior season in 2009, Kaepernick didn't have as many passing yards mostly because the team found a lot of its offensive success in the running game. In fact, Kaepernick was one of three with more than 1,000 rushing yards. The list is topped by Vail Taua (1,345 yards, 10 touchdowns), followed by Kaepernick (1,183 yards, 16 touchdowns), and Luke Lippincott (1,034, 9 touchdowns). But even though the Wolfpack was focused more on the run in their 8-5 season, Nevada's coaching staff still trusted Kaepernick to throw for 2,052 passing yards with 20 touchdowns and six interceptions. He did a little bit of everything for the Nevada offense, even catching a pass for a score.

Nevada defeated UNLV 63-28 on Oct. 3, 2009. Kaepernick caught a 6-yard touchdown pass from running back, Luke Lippincott, late in the fourth quarter in a game where he did just about everything else in the game with 208 passing yards and 173 rushing yards. In this game, he became one of only a few quarterbacks in NCAA history to throw for, run for, and catch a touchdown. It was also an important win because it came off a stretch of three straight losses to open the season.

Nevada opened the season September 5, 2009, at Notre Dame in a 35-0 loss where Kaepernick was 12-for-23 for 149 yards and two interceptions, and only 39 yards on the ground. There were equal struggles in the Wolfpack's 35-20 loss at Colorado State on September 19, 2009 where he would have 251 yards on 25 completions but had two interceptions against his one touchdown and only rushing for 24 yards. The other was in the team's 31-21 loss to Missouri on September 25, 2009. In the home opener, Kaepernick had 146 yards in the air and only 59 on the ground.

The UNLV win did not only break the three-game losing streak to start the season, it also helped turnaround a struggling Nevada offense where Kaepernick started to hit a stride of sorts. On October 9, 2009, Nevada was able to defeat Louisiana Tech 37-14 at home where Kaepernick had a hand in all of the Wolfpack's trips into the end-zone with five total touchdowns – starting with three that were within his 166 passing yards. On the ground, Kaepernick had two touchdowns within 89 yards – a majority of which came from a 67-yard run within the final moments of the third quarter to put the game out of reach of Louisiana Tech.

Having a lot of touchdowns in a game was a common theme for Kaepernick in the 2009 season where he had plenty of games where he would rush for two or three scores during an eight-game winning streak that included seven wins in the Western Athletic Conference. In his most dominant rushing performance during the Wolfpack's 70-45 win Oct. 24, 2009 against

Idaho, Kaepernick ran for 230 yards and four touchdowns, a 61-yard run in the early second quarter, and a 75-yard long run in the third quarter. He also completed 13-for-21 for 178 yards and two touchdowns.

Nevada's eight-game winning streak was snapped by their arch-nemesis from Boise State in the final game of the season on November 27, 2009 – in what would be the game to decide the WAC Championship that season. The Broncos won 44-33 where they were led by quarterback Kellen Moore's five touchdown passes. Kaepernick was able to complete only 12-of-22 passes for 141 yards and three touchdowns – he also ran for a total of 31 yards. At the end, it was Nevada's lone conference loss of the season to a Boise State team that would finish undefeated after defeating Texas Christian 17-10 in the Fiesta Bowl on January 4, 2010.

Nevada would not be able to bounce back in time for the Hawaii Bowl on December 24, 2009 – the

Wolfpack lost to Southern Methodist 45-10 where Kaepernick struggled with 15-of-29 completed passes for 177 yards and an interception. He didn't help lead an offensive touchdown drive until the last minute in the fourth quarter from a 10-yard pass to Brandon Wimberly.

**Senior Year**

Kaepernick's senior season would find himself with a big boost in his numbers as he helped Nevada to their best record in their program's history with a 13-1 season that helped them reach the 11th spot on the Associated Press Top 25 poll. It was the only time the Wolfpack program had ever finished in the poll at the end of the season. After having struggles teetering around seven and eight wins the last few years, Kaepernick came out with guns blazing in the home-opener against Eastern Washington on September 2, 2010 in a 49-24 win. Kaepernick was 26-for-37 with

306 yards and two touchdowns in the air. He also had two rushing touchdowns and 60 yards.

The next game, on September 11, 2010, Kaepernick would rush for a season-high 161 yards with two touchdowns highlighted by a 44-yard run in the first quarter in Nevada's 51-6 win over Colorado State. A week later, he would have another three touchdowns against California in a 52-31 win. These numbers would continue through the season and even include a win over the Boise State Broncos on November 26, 2010 in a matchup of then ranked No. 3 Boise State, and then No. 19 ranked Nevada in an overtime thriller 34-31.

Kaepernick was able to tie the game up in the final seconds to send the game into overtime with a 7-yard pass to Rishard Matthews as part of his 19-for-35 and 259 yard performance in the air. He also had an 18-yard touchdown run in the third quarter. It was the kind of game that allowed Nevada to finally defeat

Boise State – although both teams would claim an equal share of the WAC title since both teams finished 7-1 in their conference schedule. The lone loss for Nevada was on October 16, 2010 at Hawaii 27-21 with Kaepernick's two interceptions possibly being a big factor in the lone defeat of 2010.

It was that loss that made the difference between the Wolfpack possibly earning a spot in one of the big Bowl Championship Series bowl games – which included the Rose Bowl, Orange Bowl, Fiesta Bowl, and Sugar Bowl. But Nevada would not end the season empty-handed as they defeated Boston College 20-13 in the Fight Hunger Bowl on January 9, 2011. Kaepernick was able to complete a 27-yard pass to Matthews in the first quarter – who a few moments later would return a 72-yard punt for a touchdown.

For the second time in his collegiate career, Kaepernick would finish the season with the WAC Offensive Player of the Year Award after throwing for

3,022 passing yards with 21 touchdowns against eight interceptions – all on a 64.9 completion percentage. He also rushed for 1,206 yards and 20 additional touchdowns. Kaepernick found himself the only quarterback in the history of Division I Football Bowl Subdivision who had more than 10,000 passing yards and more than 4,000 rushing yards. He was also the first to ever have three straight seasons with more than 2,000 passing yards and more than 1,000 rushing yards.

To go along with his Bachelor's Degree in business management and a member of the Kappa Alpha Si fraternity, Kaepernick finished his time in Nevada with a total of 10,098 passing yards with 82 touchdowns against 24 interceptions and 59 rushing touchdowns on 4,112 rush yards to make him an impressive resume to enter the NFL Draft in 2011.

## MLB

Before we start getting into how Colin Kaepernick would transition from a successful senior season at the University of Nevada to jointing the National Football League, let's briefly mention that there was a very minor chance that we could have seen Kaepernick decide to turn in pads and a helmet on the football field for a pitcher's glove and rosin bag on the baseball diamond.

He was a very dominant young pitcher while growing up in Turlock High School back in California and had a few scholarship offers from NCAA Division I baseball programs. Ultimately, he would make the choice to play as a quarterback for the Wolfpack football team. Football had always been his first choice since he was eight years old, but many student-athletes in high school would rather remain active when their primary season was over. Kaepernick spent the winter months indoors playing basketball and was one of the star players with more than 12 points averaged. In the spring, he would then pitch and bat for the Pride baseball team. After high school, he made the decision to play football primarily, and he did so with the Wolfpack.

That didn't stop him from gaining some attention from Major League Baseball scouts. In his playing days at Pitman High School, he was known for a smooth pitch delivery and a fastball that reached the low-to-mid-90s range. He also had the frame of a lanky pitcher at six-foot-four and 180 pounds – he has grown a bit since then and now weighs about 230 pounds.

In his senior season at Pitman, Kaepernick had a record of 9-2 to help the Pride in the state playoffs in California where his earned runs average was 1.27 and featured nearly 100 strikeouts in just above 80 innings and had two no-hitters. Before going to Nevada, Kaepernick was one of the highest rated baseball recruits and was, in fact, receiving more offers for college baseball than football.

Despite the fact that he took an offer to play for the Nevada Wolfpack, some scouts and front office staff within the Chicago Cubs organization saw enough to warrant looking into more. They did research and the football experts in their network believed that that he wouldn't find his way into the NFL, and that was after Kaepernick had great freshman and sophomore seasons in 2007 and 2008.

The Cubs front office began to think that maybe they could get the young quarterback to change his mind on what sport he wants to play. Many quarterbacks who come from smaller programs, like Nevada and other Western Athletic Conference teams, usually will find themselves going to the less prestigious leagues like the Canadian Football League, or the Arena Football League. From the standpoint of some, selecting him in the 43rd round wasn't a risk because there are only so many players in those later rounds that can produce players who will reach the MLB roster – although it is always possible and there are exceptions to the rules.

After the selection, the team will earn the baseball rights if Kaepernick did want to play baseball and would be able to sign him. They spoke with the Colin with an offer to make between $30,000 and $50,000 to play baseball in the summer in-between school-years in Reno, Nevada. He likely would have played for one of the smaller minor league teams under the Cubs organization – like Short-Season A ball in Eugene, Oregon, or A-class ball in South Bend, Indiana.

The Cubs had a similar draft choice back in 2006 when they selected Jeff Samardzija in the fifth round of that year's draft even though he was an All-American collegiate wide receiver at Notre Dame University. Samardzija was willing to play football for the Fighting Irish and then played summer baseball with the Cubs organization. Since then, the Cubs were able to sign the former wide receiver to a long-term contract and he was able to find himself as an integral part of the Cubs' pitching rotation at the time before he found himself moved around and is now on the other side of Chicago with the White Sox. Thus, there was some successful track record of the Cubs finding someone who was willing to leave football for the baseball diamond.

It was more of a decision between making money right now and remaining focused on the dream he had that brought him to the Wolfpack. The Cubs were even willing to wait until he finished his college education and were going to entice him to use the salary he earned to cover his education costs. But the answer from Kaepernick was a polite and stern "no."

After that series of discussions back in 2009, Kaepernick would remain away from baseball. It wasn't until a few years after that he picked up a baseball for the first time in seven years when he threw the first pitch at a San Francisco Giants game on June 22, 2013. By this time, he was an NFL player for the 49ers and a lot of fans didn't know about his numbers from the small town about two hours away from the

San Francisco Bay. Back then, he had a fast ball that hovered at around 94. But in 2013, he threw a fastball at 87 miles per hour.

Maybe he could have found success in professional baseball, but he made his choice and continued to play two really good seasons and established himself as one of the best dual-threat quarterbacks in college football history. Considering the reasons the Giants invited him to throw a ceremonial first pitch at AT&T Park is likely a good sign of how his choice to pursue his dream NFL career probably went pretty good – no regrets from someone who had come off a Super Bowl XLVII about four months prior in the Mercedes-Benz Superdome in New Orleans, Louisiana.

## Chapter 4: Kaepernick's NFL Career

Months before the different front-office staff members would set up war rooms at their headquarters and inside Radio City Music Hall in New York City, Colin Kaepernick was putting on a different uniform that was uncommon from the No. 10 Nevada jersey he wore for four collegiate seasons. He still had the 2011 Senior Bowl to play on January 29, 2011 at Ladd Peebles Stadium in Mobile, Alabama – a field that also feature others who would enter the draft with high stocks, or those hoping to attract the attention of NFL teams for the first few picks where the most money can be found.

It all started with several NFL draft experts attending the practices leading up to the Senior Bowl. They commented that Kaepernick was coming in with a lot of good things to make scouts aware of him – a 3,000+ yard season, defeating the undefeated Boise State, winning the Fight Hunter Bowl against Boston

College, and having the appeal that comes with passing for more than 10,000 yards and rushing for another 4,000 in his four years with the Wolfpack. However, there were still some doubts because of throwing motion not really being what you would expect from a typical NFL quarterback and being more used to a pistol-type offense that was created by Nevada's head coach, Chris Ault.

However Colin's case was similar to how Jay Cutler was able secure himself as one of the top five quarterbacks in the 2006 NFL Draft after he had nearly 10,000 yards of total offense and had a good Senior Bowl week to become the third quarterback chosen in the draft by the Denver Broncos behind Vince Young (Tennessee) and Matt Leinert (Arizona). Kaepernick had his doubts prior to the practice in the week leading up to the Senior Bowl and part of that was beyond the negative concerns about whether he could transition to a pro-style offense.

Different draft scouts and experts were talking about the athletic abilities and history of Kaepernick. He stood at six-foot-five and was even a pitching prospect for the Chicago Cubs because of his ability to throw a fastball up to 95 miles per hour. Then they started looking more at his numbers of passing for more than 10,000 yards and 4,000 rushing yards. During the Senior Bowl, Kaepernick had a few good drives, including a 23-yard pass completion and leading a third quarter to help give the North team its first points through a field goal from kicker Kai Forbat.

**The Draft**

The next opportunity Kaepernick had to impress the scouts was the NFL Combine camp a few months later and he had some great results from what he participated in – highlighted as the fastest quarterback with a 40-yard dash time of 4.53 seconds. He also complete the 20-yard shuttle run in about 4.18 seconds and the three-cone drill in just under seven seconds

Kaepernick also did the broad jump with 115 inches, while his vertical jump was up to 32 and one-half inches.

The overview posted on the NFL's draft database wrote that he had all of the physical abilities and tools that scouts were noticing, as well as the experience in college as a competitor who could be productive and durable on the field. Because he had plenty of rushing yards with Nevada, Kaepernick had been marked as someone who could make plays with his feet if the pocket collapses so he wouldn't be forced to just take a sack and a loss of yards. His height was also a big asset because guys who stand as tall as Kaepernick are less likely to have their throws knocked down at the line.

However, there were still concerns with his ability to adapt to a pro-style offense and having to improve his accuracy. But they were still considering him as someone who would be a backup to develop in an NFL offense. On April 28, 2011, at the Radio City Music Hall in New York City, teams were prepared to make their selections among some of the best college football players sitting in attendance waiting for their chance to walk on stage to receive their new team's jersey and shake the hands with Commissioner Roger Goodell. Auburn's Cam Newton was the first overall pick to the Carolina Panthers, while Washington's Jake Locker was the second quarterback to the Tennessee Titans (eighth overall). The list would continue with Missouri's Blaine Gabbert (10$^{th}$, Jacksonville), and Florida State's Christian Ponder (12$^{th}$, Minnesota Vikings).

During the second round on that first day of the draft, Kaepernick was not among the first-round picks and he wasn't going to be one of the players who would walk onto the stage when they were selected. Instead, he was sitting at his family's home in Turlock, California, on the other end of the country. He did what a lot of players did – wait for the phone call while a camera broadcasting live through Skype announced on ESPN and the NFL Network during the live announcements. San Francisco made the call to Kaepernick before they had 49ers legend Dwight Clark announced on stage in New York. The family's reaction was shown on television; his mother embraced him with the rest cheering.

There were some talks about him being scouted by Oakland Raiders and first-year head coach, Jim Harbaugh, who took over the 49ers after leading Stanford University to the 2011 Orange Bowl over Virginia Tech. Both were entering a team that was expected to deal with growing pains after San Francisco finished 6-10 and missed the playoffs – leading to the termination of coach Mike Singletary with one game left on the schedule. There were some changes made to a West Coast offense and some work being done to give the team's quarterback from last year a better system to work for him.

Harbaugh's changes gave Smith his best season of his career as he was able to play the entire 16-game season for the first time and have 3,144 yards with 17 touchdowns and five interceptions. The 49ers were successful on the run with Frank Gore's 1,211 yards and eight touchdowns as San Francisco went from six wins in 2010 to 13 wins in 2011. They had a deep run in the playoffs where they lost to the eventual Super Bowl champion, the New York Giants, in the NFL Championship game.

It was a successful season for Smith, Gore, and the 49ers. For Kaepernick, most of his time was spent on the sidelines studying how Smith worked in the West Coast system. He made some appearances in two games for the 49ers during fill-in time where the 49ers were ahead by a wide margin, like when they defeated the Tampa Bay Buccaneers 48-3 on October 9, 2011 at Candlestick Park in San Francisco. It was one drive in the fourth quarter that went 90 yards after starting on San Francisco's 10-yard-line and lasted six minutes that concluded with running back Anthony Dixon's one-yard score to make the game 48-3. Kaepernick's 19-yard pass to Josh Morgan helped set-up the Dixon touchdown on a fourth-down – a good sign of his abilities to perform under pressure. He also had an 11-yard pass to tight end Delanie Walker and a five-yard pass to Morgan. After Tampa Bay punted late in the fourth quarter, all Kaepernick had to do was kneel on the ball twice to finish the game and gain victory for the team.

Kaepernick also earned some time in the team's 26-0 shutout victory on December 4, 2011 over NFC West Division rival, St. Louis. However, he didn't complete either of his pass attempts to Justin Peelle and Delanie Walker. He spent the playoffs learning and watching what the 49ers worked under head coach Harbaugh, offensive coordinator Greg Roman, and quarterbacks coach Geep Chryst. There was a lot to learn from Harbaugh, who spent 14 seasons in the NFL from

1987 to 2000 as a quarterback for the Chicago Bears and other teams across the league.

Harbaugh would then begin his coaching career as an assistant at Western Kentucky University and with the Oakland Raiders. He was head coach at the University of San Diego where he won a couple of Pioneer Football League championships and then made the move to Stanford where he was the coach for Andrew Luck's first year in 2009 and in 2010 – when he placed second in Heisman voting after 3,338 passing yards, 32 touchdowns, and eight interceptions. Luck also became the first overall pick of the Indianapolis Colts to take over the reins once held by veteran, and soon to be Hall of Fame quarterback, Peyton Manning.

So Harbaugh was able to use the same approaches that worked in Stanford's Palo Alto campus in California to the Bay Area where Alex Smith benefitted. Next season, Kaepernick would become the beneficiary of those coaching abilities.

## 2012 Season: Kaepernick's Emergence

After the disappointment of missing the Super Bowl, Alex Smith had plenty of success and was made the starting quarterback for the season. However, that didn't mean that Kaepernick didn't have his chance to play a dynamic role. Kaepernick scored his first NFL touchdown during the September 30, 2012 win visiting the New York Jets as he was entered into a wildcat formation and scored on a seven-yard run in the second quarter. He had four more rushed to finish the day with 50 yards for the day.

The next week, Kaepernick made some plays in the fourth quarter of a 45-3 blowout win against the Buffalo Bills where he had a 16-yard touchdown run as the main highlight. He had 39 yards on four carries as well as a seven-yard completion. But Smith was still showing signs of being the main quarterback as he was 18-for-24 for 303 yards and three touchdowns against the Bills.

In the team's 26-3 loss against the New York Giants, Kaepernick's time was limited on the field and in the 13-6 home win against the Seattle Seahawks. However, his time was about to increase by a wide margin during the team's November 11, 2012 home game against the St. Louis Rams. Smith's performance started off well in this game with a 14-yard-touchdown pass to Michael Crabtree highlighting 7-for-8 for 72 yards – but San Francisco gave up two early first quarter touchdowns to trail. However, Smith took a hit to the helmet from Rams linebacker Jo-Lonn Dunbar on the first drive shortly after that touchdown pass. He tried to rush to the left side and tried to spin to avoid the defender. Instead, Dunbar's helmet hit the back of Smith and he went down.

Because NFL teams are becoming more cautious with players being hit in the head, Smith was out for the rest of the game and this gave Kaepernick an opportunity to become the guy. Kaepernick played very well despite the game against St. Louis ended in a tie after throwing 11-for-17 for 117 yards and eight rushes for 66 yards. He had a seven-yard touchdown run in the fourth quarter and then, after a fumble on the kickoff to St. Louis, Frank Gore helped jump ahead. After scores back and forth, neither team could take control in the sudden death overtime.

Kaepernick was then given the start in Week 10 against the Chicago Bears on November 19, 2012, facing off with a defense that featured run stopping stars like linebackers Brian Urlacher and Lance Briggs, as well as defensive backs like Charles Tillman and Tim Jennings, who were known for creating turnovers. But Kaepernick found success in the air by throwing 16-for-23 for 243 yards and two touchdowns with a three-yard score to tight end Vernon Davis in the first quarter and a 10-yard pass to Crabtree in the third – en route to a 32-7 decisive victory.

In the very next week, Kaepernick led the 49ers to a 31-21 win in New Orleans over the Saints on

November 25, 2012. He was able to score a seven-yard run to draw the first blood in the game. After the game was tied, he was able to lead a touchdown drive in the third quarter that ended with a six-yard pass to running back Gore. Part of San Francisco's win was credited to the defense that was able to make plays against Saints' quarterback Drew Brees. Ahmad Brooks returned an interception from Brees' 50 yards for a touchdown to end the first half, while Donte Whitner returned an interception of his own for 42 yards. At the end of the game, Kaepernick finished with 16-for-25 for 231 yards with one touchdown and one interception, as well as six rushes for 27 yards.

This led to a little bit of a quarterback controversy between the young and dynamic quarterback that was drafted in the second round against the more veteran Smith, who had won 20 of his last 25 starts after some struggles initially in his first four seasons after being a No. 1 selection. Last season, Smith had two touchdowns and didn't turn the ball over at all to the

Giants – the team missed Super Bowl XLVI because of two untimely special team fumbles from wide receiver Kyle Williams.

But the concussion that Smith suffered against the St. Louis Rams opened the door for the young Kaepernick to show that he has the playmaking abilities to make the offensive more of a threat in hopes of finding their way to the Super Bowl with another deep playoff run – a bit of a change from Smith's style that was more of a game manager and had to fight to keep his starting job in the past. It's one thing for a head coach to want to make a change in quarterback when someone has a losing record, but San Francisco was 6-2-1 before Kaepernick was given the starting job against the Bears. Head coach Jim Harbaugh saw something special in his hand-picked quarterback from the 2011 NFL Draft and gave Colin the ball, yet there were still some growing pains.

The 49ers lost to the Rams in St. Louis on December 2, 2012 with a score of 16-13 in overtime. Kaepernick went 21-for-32 for 208 yards and nine rushes for 84 yards – including a 50-yard late in the fourth quarter in a drive that helped San Francisco jump ahead 13-10. But the Rams would tie the game up and then win it with a long Greg Zuerlein field goal. However, San Francisco would follow that up by winning three of their last four to win the division title – including a win at New England where Kaepernick threw for four touchdowns and 221 yards against the Patriots in a 41-34 win on December 16, 2012.

The 49ers earned the second seed and would get the bye week during the Wild Card round before hosting the Green Bay Packers in the NFC Division Round on January 12, 2013. It didn't start well when Kaepernick threw an interception to Green Bay's Sam Shields, who scored on a 52-yard return. Minutes later, Kaepernick was able to rebound with a drive that ended in a 20-yard touchdown run.

After an 18-yard run from Green Bay's DuJuan Harris, Kaepernick led back-to-back touchdown drives to Crabtree to put the team ahead in the second quarter. While Colin was effective in the air by throwing 17-of-31 for 263 yards, he was extremely effective on the ground with 16 rushes for 181 yards and two touchdowns. Kaepernick helped break a tie in the third quarter with a 56-yard run to give the 49ers a lead they would not give up as they defeated the Packers 45-31 to advance to the NFC Championship for the second straight season – but this time with a much more dynamic offense than the one led by Smith in the previous year. His performance of 181 rushing yards broke Michael Vick's record for rushing yards from a quarterback (173 in 2002).

Kaepernick had a pretty good game against the Atlanta Falcons as the 49ers won 28-24 on January 20, 2013 at the Georgia Dome. Kaepernick was 16-of-21 for 233 yards and did a four-yard touchdown pass to Davis to close the lead the Falcons had to only three points. But it was running back Gore who had two touchdowns in the third and fourth quarters to finish the game with 21 rushes for 90 yards. San Francisco was going to Super Bowl XLVII, where their head coach would face his brother – John – who was the head coach for the Baltimore Ravens. There was so much hype around the Harbaugh brothers facing each other in the NFL's championship game that many in the media called the game the "Harbaugh Bowl."

It was a competitive game, as one would expect, and Baltimore seemed to have their game working perfectly. Their defense forced 49ers running back LeMichael James to fumble the play that the Ravens would recover and turnaround into a touchdown drive to increase their lead to 14-3. After receiving the kickoff, Kaepernick threw an interception to Baltimore's Ed Reed that was intended for veteran wide receiver Randy Moss – the Ravens, however, weren't able to turn it into any point after turning it over on downs.

The Ravens were able to jump ahead 21-10 before halftime and on the second half kickoff, Ravens' Jacoby Jones returned the ball 108 yards for a 28-10 lead. Kaepernick was able to play much better in the second half, along with some big plays with a drive that ended with a 31-yard pass to Crabtree midway through the third quarter. After forcing the Ravens to punt from their own 9-yard-line and a San Francisco's Ted Ginn's 32 yard return, Kaepernick completed a 14-yard pass to Davis to set up Gore's six-yard run to 28-20.

The Ravens' running back Ray Rice would fumble a few minutes later that would give the 49ers the ball in Baltimore territory to set up a David Akers field goal. Kaepernick's 15-yard touchdown in the fourth quarter cut Baltimore's lead to 31-29 but the Raven's offense did just enough to manage the clock and San Francisco was not able to maintain their rhythm. In the end, they gave the Ravens and John Harbaugh the Super Bowl XLVII win. Other than the interception, Kaepernick's line was solid with 16-of-28 for 302 yards, as well as 62 yards on seven rushing attempts. But the veteran quarterback Joe Flacco gave the Ravens 22-of-33 for 287 yards and three touchdowns.

In seven starts and 13 total appearances in the regular season, Kaepernick finished the season with 1,814 passing yards, 10 interceptions and only three interceptions. But he also had a pretty impressive 415 rushing yards and five touchdowns to help give what the 49ers never had with Smith – a versatile and dynamic offense. Even with the Super Bowl loss, there was a lot to look forward to from a young, developing quarterback in Kaepernick.

## 2013 Season: The Seahawk Roadblock

When Colin Kaepernick and the San Francisco 49ers entered the 2013 season, they had a bit of chip on their shoulder. It was also a chance for the Colin to be a season-opening starting quarterback in his third season in the NFL and was going to have the reins to himself after the team traded veteran Alex Smith to the Kansas City Chiefs – ending the quarterback controversy. After the first week of the season, it looked like the 49ers were going to be a favorite to return to the Super Bowl.

On September 8, 2013, the 49ers were able to open the season with a 34-28 win over the Green Bay Packers. Kaepernick went 27-of-39 for 412 yards and three touchdowns – two to tight end Vernon Davis and one to newly acquired receiver Anquan Bolden. It's not easy to outgun the Packers' quarterback Aaron Rodgers, who went 21-of-37 for 333 yards, three touchdowns and one interception. It was a great way to start the season, until they hit a brick wall at the Century Link Field in Seattle.

Nothing really went well for Kaepernick and the rest of the 49ers' offense as they sputtered in such a way that left them sleepless in Seattle in a 29-3 loss to the Seahawks on September 15, 2013. The first sign was throwing an interception to Seahawks safety Earl Thomas after reaching Seattle's 5-yard-line in the first quarter. Moments later, in the second quarter, the 49ers' offensive lineman Bruce Miller was penalized for holding in the San Francisco end-zone – which counts as a safety to give Seattle the game's first two points.

The next time San Francisco had the ball, Kaepernick could not complete his first and second down passes before coughing up the ball in a sack that Seattle recovered to turn into three points from a field goal. As Seattle would extend its lead to 19-3, Kaepernick would throw an interception to cornerback Richard Sherman and a third in the final minutes of the fourth quarter to Kam Chancellor as Seattle ran away with a 29-3 win on primetime. Kaepernick went 13-of-28 for 127 yards and the three interceptions to Seattle's Legion of Boom.

After this game, the Seahawks would win 11 of its first 12 games to gain a big lead in the NFC West Division and the best record in the conference. Their only loss during that period was on the road in Indianapolis to the Colts 34-28 in a battle of possibly the best two quarterbacks of the 2012 NFL Draft – Seattle's Russell Wilson and Indianapolis' Andrew Luck.

Speaking of Luck and the Colts, they handed the 49ers their second loss of the season in the third week of the season on September 22, 2013 as San Francisco lost 27-7 in a game where had another tough game with 13-of-27 for 150 yards and one interception. Questions formed on whether Kaepernick was going to be like a one-hit wonder, and whether the decision to trade Smith was really such a good idea. But it was still early and there was still a chance to maintain a good pace with the Seahawks.

They stayed close with a 35-11 win at St. Louis on September 26, 2013 – a team that had tied and beat the

49ers last year. Kaepernick was 15-of-23 for 167 yards and two touchdown passes. It also helped that his running back Frank Gore also had 153 yards and one touchdown on 20 carries. It was a big monkey lifted off the back when you consider the matchups from last year. The defense was starting to find its stride as it continued to four turnovers in the team's 34-3 on October 6, 2013, against the struggling Houston Texans including three interceptions highlighted by Tramaine Brock's 18-yard return for the first points of the game. The 49ers defense did so well that Kaepernick didn't have to do much except throw 6-of-15 for 113 yards and one touchdown.

**2013 Regular Season**

After entering the bye week with a 6-2 record and one game back of the Seahawks, San Francisco did drop two straight games to the Carolina Panthers (10-9 on November 10, 2013), and at New Orleans (23-20 on November 17, 2013). They were falling fast and needed a big run to have a shot at clinching a wild card spot. The run started with wins at Washington on November 25, 2013, and at home against St. Louis on December 1, 2013.

On December 8, 2013, the 49ers were able to avenge their Week 2 loss to the Seattle Seahawks. Kaepernick went 15-of-29 for 175 yards, one touchdown and one interception. The 49ers were down by one when Gore ran past Seahawk defenders for a 51-yard run that eventually led to the game winning 22-yard field goal by Phil Dawson. Wilson attempted a deep pass to receiver Jermaine Kearse at the end of the game, but Eric Wright caught the interception to give San Francisco the win that highlighted a six-game winning streak to complete the 2013 season with a 12-4 record – Seattle won the NFC West Championship and became the top seed in the NFC playoffs with a 13-3 record.

San Francisco would have to play the role of "road warrior" to have any success in advancing to another Super Bowl, and the first stop on that road to the Vince Lombardi Trophy was in Green Bay, Wisconsin on January 5, 2014. Unlike the season-opening contest, Kaepernick went 16-of-30 for 227 yards, one touchdown and one interception. His lone score was on a 28-yard pass to David to give San Francisco a 20-17 lead in the fourth quarter – about five minutes before Green Bay kicker Mason Crosby tied the game up with a 24-yard field goal with 5:09 left. This was enough time for Kaepernick to lead a long game-ending drive where he completed long passes to Michael Crabtree of 11 and 17 yards – as well as a running for 11 yards to help set up the 33-yard Dawson field goal to give them the 23-20 win to advance.

On Jan. 12, 2014, the 49ers then went down to Charlotte, N.C., for an NFC Divisional Round match, where the 49ers kept the Carolina Panthers shutout in the second half for a 23-10 win at the Bank of America

Stadium. Kaepernick went 15-of-28 for 196 yards and 1-yard touchdown pass to Davis in the third quarter and would a few minutes later in the fourth quarter run four yards for a game clinching touchdown run.

This brings us to what would become the rubber match with the Seattle Seahawks – a team that has made Kaepernick's life very tough on the football field for multiple games. The NFC Championship game on January 19, 2014 was similarly tough for the third-year quarterback who went 14-of-24 for 153 yards with a 26-yard touchdown pass to Boldin to give the 49ers the 17-10 lead midway through the third quarter. But Seattle's offense started to pick up with running back Marshawn Lynch's 109 yards and one touchdown and Wilson throwing 16-of-25 for 215 yards and one touchdown – which came in the fourth quarter on a 35-yard pass to Jermaine Kearse.

After a 47-yard field goal by Steven Hauschka, Seattle was able to jump to a 23-17 lead with 3:37 left in the game. It was already a lot closer than the Week 2 game in Seattle and was closer to resemble the Week 14 game in San Francisco. The 49ers had the ball late in the game and Kaepernick did an eight-yard pass to Boldin and followed by an incomplete to set up a fourth-down situation, which he converted with a 17-yard pass to Gore to the San Francisco 47-yard-line. A couple of plays later, Kaepernick completed a 16-yard pass to Crabtree to move the ball to Seattle's 29-yard-line before using their first timeout.

The fans were starting to get nervous as Kaepernick completed an 11-yard pass to Davis to move the ball to Seattle's 18-yard-line. Then he made a pass to the right corner of the end zone to Crabtree – who was covered by Sherman, who made a vocal argument that he is the best cornerback in the NFL. A play at this point would elevate him to a level beyond Darrell Revis – which he did by tipping the ball away from Crabtree's hands and towards Seattle linebacker Malcolm Smith for the game-winning interception to send the Seahawks to

Super Bowl XLVIII in MetLife Stadium in New Jersey.

It wasn't a bad season from Kaepernick, just not the ending he or the 49ers nation were hoping for. If it was any consolation, he completed 58.4 percent for 3,197 yards, 21 touchdowns and eight interceptions, as well as running the ball 92 times for 524 yards and four touchdowns. But he and the rest of the team would sit at home and watch the Seahawks face Peyton Manning in the Super Bowl – a game where the Seahawks dominated in a 43-8 victory. It meant the team would have to bounce back and make improvements in the hope of getting back to the championship game.

**2014 Season: A Step in the Wrong Direction**

When a team makes three straight appearances in the NFC Championship and one Super Bowl appearance, the expectations can be quite high among the fan base. So when a team starts to digress a little bit, there are a lot of concerns for the entire offense, and that would include a star quarterback like Colin Kaepernick. But the start was very similar to the last year when they finished 12-4 and only behind the Seahawks for the best record in the NFC.

On September 7, 2014, the 49ers earned a road win against the Dallas Cowboys 28-17. This is thanks in part to a 21-point run in the first quarter that gave them a lead they were able to hold onto the rest of the contest. Defensive back Chris Culliver returned a fumble for 35 yards and a touchdown, followed by two touchdown passes from Kaepernick to tight end Vernon Davis of 29 and 2 yards respectfully – who would finish the game with 16-of-23 for 201 yards. It was a powerful win that gave the fans a lot of hype with the team hosting the Chicago Bears who had one of the worst defensive units the year before.

The 49ers led their home opening game 20-7, entering the fourth quarter in a game where Kaepernick finished the game with 21-of-34 for 248 yards and a 3-

yard touchdown pass to Michael Crabtree. But the quarterback struggled with turnovers in the game that included an interception to Chris Conte and a fumble to Jared Allen to keep Chicago in the match. But Chicago's quarterback Jay Cutler led a touchdown drive to receiver Brandon Marshall to make it 20-14 San Francisco. Kaepernick would then throw an interception to rookie cornerback Kyle Fuller to help set up a 3-yard pass from Cutler to tight end Martellus Bennett. Minutes later, another Kaepernick interception to Fuller would set up a go-ahead touchdown pass from Cutler to Marshall and the Bears defeated San Francisco 28-20.

The 49ers would then drop a game in Arizona on September 21, 2014, in a 23-14 loss to the Cardinals who were looking to be the breakout team of the 2014 season by winning nine of their first 10 games of the season. Drew Stanton wasn't even the team's top quarterback as Carson Palmer was out due to an injury. Still, he threw 18-of-33 for 244 yards and two touchdowns. Kaepernick didn't throw any interceptions as he was 29-of-37 for 245 yards and a 2-yard touchdown pass to Michael Crabtree. It was just a great game from Arizona and a case of missed opportunities for the San Francisco offense.

The 49ers would win their next three games, starting with a 26-21 win at home against the Philadelphia Eagles on September 28, 2014, where Kaepernick would go 17-of-30 for 218 yards and two touchdowns that included a 55-yard pass to running back Frank Gore. Kaepernick would get a good performance in his first game against former teammate Alex Smith, who was now the quarterback for the Kansas City Chiefs. Colin would go 14-for-26 for 201 yards and a 9-yard pass to Steve Johnson. Smith struggled as he went 16-of-30 for 158 yards and one touchdown, and one interception.

Things started to feel better with the offense coming together when the 49ers defeated St. Louis Rams 31-

17 on October 13, 2014. But their next two games were losses, starting with a 42-17 loss in Denver on October 19, 2014, with Kaepernick throwing 24-for-39 for 263 yards, one touchdown and one interception. His counterpart was the elder veteran, Peyton Manning, who went 22-of-26 for 318 yards and four touchdowns. Even after a bye week, the 49ers lost to the St. Louis Rams at home on November 2, 2014. While Kaepernick went 22-of-33 for 237 yards and one touchdown, the 49ers could not get any offense going and were shutout in the second half. In fact, San Francisco only totaled 263 yards and almost nothing on the ground, which had been such a strong point for the team in the past years.

There was a glimmer of hope as the 49ers won their next three games, starting with an overtime win at New Orleans on November 9, 2014 with a score of 27-24. Kaepernick completed less than half of his passes at 14-of-32 but still had 210 yards and a 15-yard touchdown to Anquan Boldin. They were able to follow it up with a 16-10 win in New York to defeat the Giants on November 16, 2014. Kaepernick was 15-of-29 for 193 yards and a 48-yard touchdown pass to Crabtree to give the team the lead they would hold onto for the rest of the game. Kaepernick would look strong on November 23, 2014 at home against the Washington Redskins in a 17-13 win where he would throw 20-29 for 256 yards and one touchdown pass to Boldin for 30 yards in the first quarter.

While there were struggles and concerns, the 49ers were still fighting for a Wild Card playoff spot with a home game a few days later for Thanksgiving. Unfortunately they found themselves facing the Seattle Seahawks in a primetime game. Just like other games with Seattle, Kaepernick struggled as he was 16-of-29 for only 121 yards. Seattle cornerback Richard Sherman intercepted a first quarter pass from Kaepernick, who would also throw to the Seahawk in jersey No. 25 again late in the fourth quarter as Seattle dominated in a 19-3 win. Russell Wilson was responsible for the game's lone touchdown in a 13-yard pass to running back Robert Turbin early in the game.

Many 49ers fans were hoping to get a quick turnaround in their next game with the struggling Oakland Raiders who only had one win going into the December 7, 2014 showdown between the Bay Area teams. However, this single turned into two as the Raiders defeated the 49ers 24-13. Kaepernick had an 8-yard touchdown pass to lineman Bruce Miller, which was the lone touchdown for San Francisco. Kaepernick finished 18-of-33 for 174 yards. His first throw was an interception by Oakland defender Brendian Ross. He would then throw another with two minutes left in the game when Oakland's Charles Woodson helped clinch the game for the Raiders.

Along with the Thanksgiving Day loss to Seattle at home, the 49ers were starting a very long losing streak that would continue in Seattle with a 17-7 loss to the

Seahawks on December 14, 2014, where Kaepernick would go 11-for-19 with only 141 yards total with no touchdowns either through the air or on the ground.

It looked like the 49ers were going to snap the loss in a December 20, 2014 home game against the San Diego Chargers where Kaepernick went 15-of-24 for 114 yards and one touchdown. But his main contributions came from running with the ball and having 151 yards on seven carries that were highlighted by a 90-yard run to put the 49ers up 35-21 in the third quarter

But San Diego's Phillip Rivers led a couple of touchdown drives, starting with a 21-yard pass to tight end Antonio Gates with just a little more than five minutes left in the game. After getting the ball back, Rivers would tie the game with an 11-yard pass to receiver Malcolm Floyd and send it into overtime. San Francisco started with the ball before running back Quinton Patton fumbled after running for 20 yards, and the ball came out and was recovered by the Chargers'

Sean Lisselmore. Rivers would then lead a drive that set up a 40-yard field goal by Nick Novak to win 38-35.

If it was any consolation, the 49ers were able to win the final game of their season by playing spoiler to the Arizona Cardinals 20-17 to keep them from winning the NFC West Division – which was once again claimed by the Seattle Seahawks. Kaepernick was 15-of-26 for 204 yards and threw a 76-yard touchdown pass to Boldin in the first quarter. Kaepernick led a third quarter drive with runs of 30 and 15 yards to help set up a 3-yard touchdown run to Bruce Miller that would become the game-winning score of the game.

For a team that had three straight appearances in the NFC Championship game and one appearance in the Super Bowl, the fan base in Niner Nation was hurt by how they fell to 8-8. Kaepernick completed 60.5 percent of his passes for 3,369 yards, 19 touchdowns and 10 interceptions. He also rushed for 639 extra yards and one rushing touchdown. It was a tough feeling for Kaepernick who would not see playoff action for the first time of his career. He would watch from home as their division rival, Seattle Seahawks, would make their second straight Super Bowl appearance.

If it was any consolation, San Francisco's biggest rival lost the Vince Lombardi Trophy to the New England Patriots after a last minute interception from Russell Wilson to give the Patriots the championship.

# Chapter 5: Colin Kaepernick's Legacy and Future

The 2014 season was not the best team to debut in their newly built Levi's Stadium – which is actually located in Santa Clara, California, a short drive from San Francisco. After a tough season where they missed the playoffs after three straight NFC Championship games, a lot of people left the team. Weeks after the final game of the season, head coach Jim Harbaugh announced that he would be leaving the team to take on the coaching position at his alma mater, the University of Michigan.

Jim Tomsula would then be hired to take over the coaching reins of the 49ers after spending four seasons as the defensive line coach. Geep Chryst, who has been the quarterbacks coach working with Colin Kaepernick since he was drafted in 2011, was named San Francisco's offensive coordinator. This could be a move where the 49ers can design an offense that works more on Kaepernick's strengths to make plays on his feet. He'll also have a few new weapons on his team including wide receiver Torrey Smith and running back Reggie Bush.

However, long-time San Francisco running back Frank Gore left the team and signed a contract with the Indianapolis Colts, and receiver Michael Crabtree left and signed a new contract with the Oakland Raiders. However, San Francisco's big problem upon entering the 2015 season are the defensive issues, with the loss of cornerbacks Chris Culliver and Perrish Cox in free agency, and the retirement of linebacker Patrick Willis and Chris Borland.

It's too early to assume one way or another how the 49ers will do in the 2015 season, but there's no doubt that Kaepernick has a lot of potential to be a successful quarterback in his own right within the 49ers' illustrious history. However, that doesn't mean he's likely to become the greatest quarterback in franchise history – not with names like Joe Montana, with four Super Bowl rings, and Steve Young, with one.

Neither Montana nor Young had the type of footwork and running abilities that Kaepernick brings to the red and gold. However, he's had a number of games where he struggled to throw more than 200 yards in a game. Moving forward, Kaepernick will have to first start finding a way to address the Seattle Seahawks and their defense highlighted by the Legion of Boom, which have become a roadblock of sorts for the 49ers since 2012.

Time will tell how Kaepernick falls into the all-time comparisons of San Francisco quarterbacks, but the first step for him is to learn the new offense designed by Tomsula and Chryst.

## Final Word/About the Author

I was born and raised in Norwalk, Connecticut. Growing up, I could often be found spending many nights watching basketball, soccer, and football matches with my father in the family living room. I love sports and everything that sports can embody. I believe that sports are one of most genuine forms of competition, heart, and determination. I write my works to learn more about influential athletes in the hopes that from my writing, you the reader can walk away inspired to put in an equal if not greater amount of hard work and perseverance to pursue your goals. If you enjoyed *Colin Kaepernick: The Inspiring Story of One of Football's Greatest Quarterbacks* please leave a review! Also, you can read more of my works on *Aaron Rodgers, Peyton Manning, Tom Brady, LeBron James, Kyrie Irving, Klay Thompson, Anthony Davis, Stephen Curry, Kevin Durant, Russell Westbrook, Chris Paul, Blake Griffin, Joakim Noah, Scottie Pippen, Kobe Bryant, Carmelo Anthony, Kevin Love,*

*Grant Hill, Tracy McGrady, Vince Carter, Patrick Ewing, Karl Malone, Tony Parker, Allen Iverson, Hakeem Olajuwon, Reggie Miller, Michael Carter-Williams, James Harding, John Wall, Tim Duncan,* and *Steve Nash* in the Kindle Store. If you love basketball, check out my website at [claytongeoffreys.com](claytongeoffreys.com) to join my exclusive list where I let you know about my latest books and give you lots of goodies.

## Like what you read?

I write because I love sharing the stories of influential athletes like Colin Kapernick with fantastic readers like you. My readers inspire me to write more so please do not hesitate to let me know what you thought by leaving a review! If you love books on life, basketball, or productivity, check out my website at claytongeoffreys.com to join my exclusive list where I let you know about my latest books. Aside from being the first to hear about my latest releases, you can also download a free copy of *33 Life Lessons: Success Principles, Career Advice & Habits of Successful People.* See you there!

# Bibliography

1. Dahlberg, Tim. "Column: Painful Losses Endure for Kaepernicks." *AP Online*. N.p., 1 Feb. 2013. Web.

2. Himmelsbach, Adam. "Not a Household Name, Not Even in Nevada." *The New York Times*. The New York Times, 28 Aug. 2010. Web.

3. "Various Sources." *MaxPreps.com*. N.p., n.d. Web.

4. Knapp, Gwen. "Strange but True Tales of Colin Kaepernick." *SportsonEarth.com*. N.p., n.d. Web. 25

5. "Various NFL, college football Sources." *Sports-Reference.com*. N.p., n.d. Web.

6. "The Story behind the Cubs Drafting 49ers Quarterback Kaepernick." *CSN Chicago*, 12 Dec. 2012. Web.

7. Conway, Tyler. "Kaepernick's 1st Pitch Hits 87." *Bleacher Report*. N.p., 22 June 2013. Web.

8. Levine, Bruce. "Cubs Couldn't Sway Colin Kaepernick." ESPN. *ESPN Internet Ventures*, 23 Jan. 2013. Web.

9. Garrison, Jason. "Super Bowl 2013: Colin Kaepernick's NFL Journey Started at the Senior Bowl."*SBNation.com*. N.p., 26 Jan. 2013. Web.

10. "NFL Events: Combine Player Profiles - Colin Kaepernick." *NFL Events: Combine Player Profiles - Colin Kaepernick*. N.p., Mar. 2011. Web.

Printed in Great Britain
by Amazon